WORDS
OF
A FEATHER

THE MYSTIC MUSINGS
OF A MEDICAL MAN

DR. JFW NDIKUM

Order this book online at www.trafford.com
or email orders@trafford.com

Most Trafford titles are also available at major online book retailers.

Print information available on the last page.

ISBN: 978-1-4907-7613-2 (sc)
ISBN: 978-1-4907-7615-6 (hc)
ISBN: 978-1-4907-7614-9 (e)

Library of Congress Control Number: 2016913305

Trafford rev.   08/27/2016

 www.trafford.com
North America & international
toll-free: 1 888 232 4444 (USA & Canada)
fax: 812 355 4082

Dedicated with Love,
To the Infinite Within

Dear John,

Thank you so much for all the support over the last couple of years. May life shower you with the same blessings you have given others... and more.

Your friend

John S

PREFACE

This four-part collection of poems chronicles a tumultuous and intense phase in my life. Dashed into the throes of life – its ecstasies and its agonies – and a close witness (in my work as a medical doctor) to the human condition, I found solace in expressing the restless inferno raging within my psyche.

The poems were written as they 'arrived', sometimes after ward-rounds and frequently on public transport. Occasionally, they would arrive in the shower, forcing me to leap out and rapidly pen whatever words did 'flash upon that inward eye', before they vanished into nothingness. I wrote on inspiration and the objects of my reflection always proved a most wonderful muse.

This period - despite its insufferable upheavals - has blessed me with lessons that I shall cherish for the rest of my life. I hope you shall enjoy (or gladly suffer) reading the poems as much as I did witnessing them flow from the mysterious Kingdom Within.

Warmest blessings to you dear reader.

Dr. JFW Ndikum
July 2016
Gaucin, Spain

Made weak by time and fate, but strong in will
To strive, to seek, to find, and not to yield.

Alfred, Lord Tennyson

CONTENTS

• INITIATION 1

1. Phoenix 5
2. Love's Shore 6
3. The Making of A Muse 7
4. Love 8
5. Divinations 10
6. Fishes 11
7. Songs of Ecstasy 12
8. Blessed Misfortune 13
9. Blush 14
10. Done 15
11. Anahata 17
12. You Are 18
13. Fathomless 20
14. The Day Two Psyches Kissed 21
15. A Mid-Morning Muse 22
16. Voyeur 23
17. Poet's Delight 24
18. Hearts' Spar 25
19. Stunner 28
20. Beauty-Sweet 29
21. The Composer 30
22. Oh, Beauty! 31
23. Insatiable 32
24. You 33

25. Poet of Arabia 34
26. Adoration Arising 35
27. You My Deliverer 36
28. No Return 37
29. Oh, To Dream of Thee 38
30. Match 39
31. My Sweet Rose 40
32. Remembering Amy Winehouse 41
33. Gezellig 42
34. The Middle Way 43
35. The Essence of Writ 44
36. The Fifth Kingdom 45
37. Sacred Awe 46
38. Ménage à Deux 47
39. Oh, Intuition 48
40. He Composes Writ; or, an Ode to Cosmic Intelligence 49
41. Wisdom's Land 51
42. Dust of the Ancients 52
43. Egypt's Rise 53
44. The Royal Art 55
45. Kundalini Tidings 56
46. Serpent Power 57
47. Aurum Potabile 58
48. It Consumeth Me: an Ode to Alchemy 59
49. Oh, Alchemy 61
50. The Dragon 63
51. Mystic's Biology 65
52. Buddha the Neuroscientist 66
53. Altruism True 67
54. Oh Man! 68
55. The Venus Project 69
56. Lincoln's Lantern 70
57. The Fourth Commandment 72
58. Why Wait 74
59. Gnothi Seauton 75
60. Oh, Capitalist 76

61. Lost 77
62. The Slave 78
63. We Blind Men 79

• DESPAIR 81

64. Oh, Woman! 85
65. Habibti 87
66. Goodbye My Lover 89
67. Why Big Boys Never Tell 92
68. Tell Me Friend 93
69. When 94
70. Bipolar 96
71. Badass 98
72. On Missing You 99
73. Shades of Black 100
74. Her Sin 102
75. Retrospectoscope 103
76. Dreams 104
77. Divine Discontent 105
78. My Pilgrimage 106
79. Patient's Son 108
80. Guardian Angel 110
81. Oh, Hospital 111
82. Medicine and Philosophy 112
83. Senior Be Kind; or, a Junior Doctor Speaks 113
84. Patients' Ache 115
85. 4am 117
86. Teardrop 118
87. Ambition's Sin 119
88. Delusionals 120
89. My Song 121
90. Of Heaven Dream 122
91. Golgotha 123
92. A Young Poet's Lament 124
93. Human Nature; or, My Most Painful Lesson Yet 125
94. Me 126

95. Pensive.. 127
96. The Modern Poet... 128
97. The Poets' Fate.. 129
98. All is Fair... 130
99. Naivety's Child... 131
100. Russian Roulette.. 132
101. What is Life?.. 133
102. Little John... 134
103. Tired.. 135
104. Undreaming... 136
105. Nude.. 137
106. A Poet Spent.. 138
107. The Second Birth.. 139

• HOPE!..141

108. My Atman..145
109. Spiritual Warrior... 146
110. Where There's a Will...147
111. Beauty; Or, The Curse.. 148
112. Chrysalis.. 150
113. Illumination...151
114. Prodigal... 152
115. Arena Terra...153
116. My Queen... 154
117. Phoenix Rising... 155
118. 4th Night... 156
119. Follow Nature... 157
120. Epiphany.. 158
121. Fortitudas.. 159
122. New Age... 160
123. I Remember..161
124. Perseverantia..162
125. He Visions This...163
126. Peg-Leg.. 164
127. The Duel.. 165
128. Sensei's Lesson... 166

129. Recess À-La Ginsberg 167
130. Lothario 168
131. Inner Pain 170
132. Dreams..171
133. Think On These Things...172
134. Neither Black Nor White 173
135. Freedom Won 174
136. That Lion-Force 175
137. An Ode to Maslow 176
138. Tat Tvam Asi.. 177
139. Beseeched...179
140. Dichotomy 180
141. The Day Heaven Spoke..181
142. An Ode to the Master Alchemist 182
143. That Girl 183
144. But a Dream 184
145. Sea of Diamonds.. 186
146. That Secret Strength... 187

• LIGHT 189

147. Immortal Deeds.. 193
148. Lessons of Hades 194
149. Tomorrow's Man.. 195
150. Know This 196
151. Hyperspace; or, the Music of the Spheres 197
152. Ambrosia.. 198
153. Apprenticed to Thee 199
154. Sacred Duty..200
155. The Poet's Clover 201
156. SMALL 'p' pHILOSOPHY 202
157. J'espère.. 203
158. Unrooted..204
159. An Epiphany...205
160. Sweet Freedom, Ring! 206
161. Self-Compassion 207
162. My Nirvanas...208

163. Subterfuge...209
164. An Ode to Nature 210
165. Poets Arise!...211
166. Sun-Tuition...212
167. On True Marriage 213
168. A Prayer 214
169. Our Harvest, ...215
170. The Alchemist; or, Autobiography of a Poet............................216

PART I

INITIATION

It begins as an effulgence of bliss; a showering of love that at first appears to come from without and is later recognised as emerging from within. The psyche - peeking through a new aperture - waltzes in the splendour of the 'divine-lit blaze'. Nothing can go wrong. Or so it seems. Although we do not yet realise it, this taste of the Light is our incentive to begin walking the ageless Inward Path.

PHOENIX

The Poet in me
He dormant lay,
Lost in the midst of Life's bleak play.
Anon - His heart was stirred by a new Light
And boldly, He re-emerged with fervent new
might!

LOVE'S SHORE

What wondrous ferments do arise
When poets from their skilled pens write
Such splendid verses that ignite
Young hearts and make young lovers wise.

This talk of blessed divine oars
And spirit transformation lore,
Shall make meek youth so evermore
Thirsty to boat to other shores.

So enjoin now in fine array,
Let eager pens to paper meet;
Rejoice in moments ever sweet
And in your pastured verses, rested, lay.

It is
Your inexplicable
Supernal Light
That sets Poets' hearts alight.
A Natural beauty that leaves us in a daze,
For it does
Quite simply,
Amaze.

LOVE

When kindred souls together wind
Through supple fingers intertwin'd;
In sweet ambrosial currents lay
And to each other softly pray.

Do these young lovers rested near
Have slightest inkling, even here
That what does softly between them flow
Is the essence by which all things grow:

The seed of trees, and stars at night,
The force that sets the sun alight
And hailstorms falling, 'tis the hand
That brings them fore, from distant land.

The tune that does from fair lark play
To bring light to e'en the darkest day;
When all at once seemed ever bleak
Lifts you to fairest cloud brushed peak!

But man with his constricted mind
Does even now, seek out to find
A word that does this marvel explain,
And make the Infinite seem plain.

But how can we all reckon that
The Lord, donned in a glory hat
(Who does fine worlds with thinking sculpt
And by His wish, mountains erupt)

Should be so easy to conceive,
When we can't even here receive
His love into our feeble hearts -
And our wars, still, we think are arts.

When he but wishes we could surrender'd, stand
And take cherished time to understand
That He is Love, and Love is He
And He resides, in all of thee.

DIVINATIONS

'Tis admiration's divinations
That give rise to sublime inspirations -
Give praise, I do now decree;
This is the way, we Poets shall be set free.

FISHES

We live
And breathe
In an Ocean of Love -
And still we know it not.

Held aloft
On this Earth-ephemeral-string,
Where sure destruction seems our lot.

But amidst the waves
Of
Merciless Tides
Men known as poets, oft do glimpse
Beyond the veil of the mortal shroud,
And their bounty
Share Selflessly.

SONGS OF ECSTASY

My soul sings songs of ecstasy
And Nature echoes in glee;
This rapture-laden spirit entranced
In swoon - as if it'd never been free.

And high-basked in Her crimson sunsets
Whereupon my true-Mind doth rest.
This soul sings songs of ecstasy
'Til Nature echoes in glee!

BLESSED MISFORTUNE

Must this short life be so prosaic,
Nay! Let's make it all mosaic.
For though life's trials so nefarious
Seem, they seek only to prepare us

For a life divine, where immortals dine
On a fine ambrosial wine;
Enjoying heaven's fruitful symphony,
And its wondrous melody

BLUSH

You did just warm my heart enough for it
To melt the sun;
Causing me to frolic and bask,
In abstract,
Poesic pun.

DONE

When spiritual seekers' talents bloom
And Samadhi transformation looms,
Heaven gloss'd by sweetest Providence
Brought to fore - radiant effervescence
That does from waking third eye flow.
A secret the learned have yet to know,
Forever blinded in their high conceit,
'Tis wretched fate they soon shall meet
For denying Heaven's warnings
And insisting on their leanings
Towards materialistic doctrines' down here spate
They shall bring down an awful fate.
Knowing not man's bod' a Temple be
And a glorious future it shall see;
Earthly denizens shall soon jet
To Eden, once by sacred serpent set.
And 'Vakri', yes an unknown flow
They too, shall soon be wont to know
My words, high-horsed, yes they may seem
Do not this all so harshly deem.

For though to you it makes no sense,
I do provide sweet evidence
That kundalini transformation
Be reality - and do dream of a Nation
Where tended kin shall learn its teachings
And treasures here, learn all its meanings.
And though now fit victims for your scorn,
These god-men the world shall soon adorn
With beauties Earth has never seen
And wonders that have never been;
A human race, full grown - mature,
Guided by kind Nature's azure.
And now my work here has been done
To show I am not the only one
Who, when by secret fire gifted
Can be to sweet Jove's Kingom lifted

ANAHATA

When those mystic petals by Light's flame unfold,
He doth whisper under bated breath what should
not be told;
For all thoughts of virtue did nigh from him depart
On a night that was truly, an Art.

YOU ARE

I felt it today:
A love that never was, and shall never be,
But always Is.
Ecstatic streams of wisdom
Did serenely drip onto the lips of my intuition
As I contemplated this.
You - the serenity of my being.
And me,
Yours.

What can compare to a love Eternal
That laughs - unabashedly -
At time.
And space.
Can there exist anything more wondrous
More bountiful
More joyous
More free.
Even, perhaps, more precious.

Impossible.

And I daren't make a mockery of this
Cosmic emanation
That is Love;
Woe to such Blasphemy.
And its treacherous ways.

To deny Love -
Would be to deny you
Mon amour.
Do you not see me lost in contemplation
At a love that knows not
Space,
Nor time.
'Til swung into the throes of this Cosmic song,
I hear Eternity declare:
"She is the serenity of His being.
And he
Is, Forever -
Hers".

FATHOMLESS

What untapped potential doth reside
Beyond Man's intellectual pride?
When I did that moment into your Psyche gaze,
I knew You
And all of your days.

THE DAY TWO PSYCHES KISSED

Just one soular gaze,
And you knew me
And I knew you.
And that, my dear,
Was It.

A MID-MORNING MUSE

Ah, ye fair maidens, how I adore you so!
You feel as deeply, as any poet.
Know that when from my heart, sweet-rhyme does
flow -
'Tis, you my dears, that've inspired such sonnets.

VOYEUR

Who does the poets' language speak
Can, into his very Spirit, peek.

POET'S DELIGHT

The Black Poet in London's twilight
Reveals now what he by day conceals;
His Inner might,
A true-essence
Veiled from his compatriots' sight.
All the while,
By inner sensoria
He revels in Dionysian
Flight.

HEARTS' SPAR

When by her presence he was bade
To this sweet mistress serenade,
A sweet song from his heart did sing,
Echoing Vivaldi's strings.
Gripped by her beauty - heavenly -
He did try fervently to keep
His feelings, deep from being revealed.
And swore then, to keep them veiled.

See:
Such sweetness from her voice did flow,
The sun radiant, from her eyes did glow -
Her skin its velvet he could secretly sense
And her heart did throb, with life.
Those ovals of her eyes as globes
Surpassing earth's lunar splendours
Her mere visage - its symmetry,
A pure mystery;
For how could such perfection be.

She did advance,
His heart did bound
His ears filling with its rhythmic sound.
But outwardly, he remained
Non-chalant
And softly spake thus,
"Hi".

She too, it seems
Appeared unfazed
Judging - as he did - by her face.
Nevertheless, she greeted him
Warmly,
And his heart - he felt it slowly warm.

He struck a pose
Leant back and further still
Tilted his body
From
Her own, so that
His intention – although now clear -
Would somewhat, ambiguous, be.

"Wherefrom',
Enquired he gently
'Does a maiden sweet
As thee, my fairest,
Hail?
How can such beauty
On this mortal ground exist,
Yet I never found its trail?"
She smiled, spake her Motherland's name
And he knew from where she came.
"Ah yes", said he
"I know of it
A great poet of acclaim,
Did from that very land spring!"

They much longer spake,
Timelessness passed
High laughter together they did share.
Two strangers' meet
Almost heaven sent,
Hearts skipping to harmony's beat.

Now comforted
The two hearts melodiously
sparred, chiming to Cupid's duet.
Teasing - a smile,
Flirting - a frown,
Enjoying it all the while.

Alas - that time did come
To overcome
The – speeded minutes' – rapport.
And his heart did ache,
Yet he did again fake
A full-felt non-chalance.
Since women from their eyes do speak,
Through them he did her soul softly kiss.
And knew then, he'd danced with a soul
He'd soon painfully miss.

STUNNER

Your beauty doth make
Other maidens seem pale.
Their smile,
In comparison,
Stale.
A Fatal look that does somehow derail,
The focused mind of an intellectual male.

BEAUTY-SWEET

'Tis you
My dear,
Being beauteous,
That doth make beauty sweet.

THE COMPOSER

Music and verse be intertwined;
The manna that does spirit feed.
Their ferments be the very seed
Of that wine
'Pon which the Immortals dine.

OH, BEAUTY!

She doth awake my Spirit's flame
That of late, has here laid tame.
With beauty that does a mortal stun
'Til desires to Mt. Olympus run
Where those of her kind,
Enchanted
Dwell
Supping from the Ambrosial well.
To rise in beauty with each passing day, and grace
Our dreams - this Immortal Race.

And once perchance
In each blue moon,
Its beings do descend
Upon the mortal plane
To share
That glow 'pon which Poets depend.
And so our tender hearts awake,
Its fruit – this lovestruck writ.
Friends, what can we of our Creator make,
Who sculpts with such ingenious wit.

INSATIABLE

Love songs do tend
To sweep rapture-rend
Sweethearts into an inexplicable
Love, insatiable.

YOU

Meeting you
Has been such a joy;
Has set my young soul free.
How can I ever again claim to be in want,
When blessed by this: Heaven's decree.

POET OF ARABIA

When she did pen such beauteous verse
To match writ with her name.
The Heavens - awestruck - did unclose and
Swift showered her with fame.

ADORATION ARISING

I oft wonder whether men be blind
Or are possessed of malfunctioning minds,
When they miss beauty so very fair;
Eyes at which I cannot help -
But stare.
And when by this strange motion wrought
I do my childish shyness,
Mask.
And compose writ in secret whence,
I do - as a wise man -
In your Glory
Bask.

YOU MY DELIVERER

My thought did right now toward you stray,
I have this entire night awake stayed
And pondered deep life's meaning 'til,
It made my mind stand still.
Yet suffused deep with pranic-Light,
It took all of my mental might
To reason from this plight.
'Til
Thought did softly to'ard you glide
Leaving me glee filled,
Oh -
What a majestic flight.
A sojourn I shall in my bosom keep;
My sweet deliverer's Light.

NO RETURN

Sweet feelings he had once forsworn
To banish from his jilted range,
Now full force -as if by Cupid's scorn -
Do return here
Swift!
And a poet, who when anguished lain did vow
To seal his crispened heart, now wonders how
Her radiance; this young maiden's glow
Secretly into his entombed heart did flow.
Numstruck, aye, yet he rises still
And from soul's hill glimpses love true.
Pacing, fearful at every step
Of a love, that may know no return.

OH, TO DREAM OF THEE

Anon!
We'll bathe in sweetest revelries,
Our thirsting lips uttering, soothing profanities.
Oh - let now this clay I wear, swift vanquished be,
Lest telepaths, my cloistered day-dreaming see.
I feign, my might 'tis nought,
It cannot fight
She,
Who doth o'er
My kneeling heart reign.
So let no word I say here be reneged,
Aye - let this song today rule sovereign.

MATCH

When the mere thought of someone
Seems to give
You,
A peace of mind unmatched.
Leaving you to wonder whether it be,
The two of you be matched.

MY SWEET ROSE

My dear lass:
Thou art to me ever new,
And do nightly my spirit renew.
This very night after I had with Jove himself convers'd
'Tis for you alone that I did sing in verse.

In brooding, brooded I,
'Til my brooding died
For thinking upon what more I could
In your magnificence find.
Sweet rose you are to me ever new,
And knowing you, mine life has been wholly renewed.

REMEMBERING AMY WINEHOUSE

I am so struck in horror
By the death of Amy Winehouse and the terror
Of these frequent deaths;
I wish her soul a blessed rest

In Heaven where its pleasant tune
May dress her, and up on the moon
She'll prance in high regalia,
To be adorned for sweet millenia

By stars on pillowed sky that sprinkle
And when wishes are made, do softly tinkle.
You graced the world with a gracious voice
And of your birth, we all rejoice

That talent born down here on Earth
Can in moment's touch, free us from dearth;
You suffered, but a finest gift
You lent us - may your rest be sweet.

GEZELLIG

How oft men waste their lives away
Assuming they'll win another day.
How oft men are so wont to say
"I'll do all this all another day".

But.

Another day may never come
And short moments that do match the sum
Of lifetimes' worths that we are lent,
Are by modern hectics rarely wisely spent.

So -

I listened to an ailing young man's tale;
Absorbed his wisdom and rejoiced
That despite his moments ever frail,
He taught sweet Truth of Heaven's voice

THE MIDDLE WAY

I trod upon the Middle Way
And found it to be evolution's path -
'Tis too absurd, some may now say,
But silence on this I wish to keep lest wrath
Of God I do incur
And wretched misfortune does occur.
But through words to me, now here lent
Lies a message I am told must be sent
To stubborn armies of our day,
Who fail to heed to kind Nature's Way
But soon as if by divine foray
Death shall on our doorstep lay
To make this century's hard-headed clan
Take sweet good time to understand
There lies far more than our current senses show,
This lesson Nature shall make sure we know
To silence those whose pomp and show
Does naught to serve their brethren here
And from whose mouths only vices flow
For all they do is jab and jeer.
So listen now men of our day
Ignore not these words, I do pray
For they flow in times of urgent need.
Such is our time - men, do take heed!

One word acts as the very Seed
From which a poem grows;
One word- the mystic stream
It seems,
Of profuse poesic flow.

THE FIFTH KINGDOM

Wherefrom does this essence in me flow?
I do daily feel its presence grow,
So I may sprinkle sheets with Heaven's air
And sweet rhythmic song so ever fair.

Ne'er did I dream I would a poet be,
Nor an artist's life did I forsee,
But this Grecian fountain does in me spring
And my elated soul gloriously sings.

For this 'holy water' makes its presence felt
E'en when by life's harshest blows dealt;
Immortal, pure, immune from pain,
This soular jewel has for aeons in silence lain.

And as I further tread evolution's path
I taste the bitter sorrow of karma's wrath
But still, am blessed with poesic flow
That does brighter than one-thousand suns glow.

And now know mystic's tale, it be no myth
Those wise men, see, what then they did
Can be, by each mortal here achieved
'Til humankind reaches heights it ne'er could have
e'en conceived.

SACRED AWE

By the waters of life am I daily cleansed
When wisdom doth in my single eye flow.
In such moments 'tis such divine beauty sensed
That I do nought but bask in its empyrean glow.

MÉNAGE À DEUX

Intuition is the fount
From which my poems flow.
And my intellect
The dutiful hands,
By which they gently grow.

OH, INTUITION

As a growing poet who
In school did writing resist,
It astounds me how little
Is understood Intuiton, that does truly exist.

The still and quiet vacant shrill
That does beyond the senses thrill.
The whisper that, 'as if from nowhere stems'
To bless with verse, the facile pen.

The 'Daemon' of with Socrates spoke,
That meets with men even in brooks.
Whose bated breath does daily conspire
To find itself in their perfumed books.

The Sergeant's warning from afar,
The morning glory star
That warned Churchill, of that impending doom
"Maids and cooks! Quick! Empty the room!"

And even the financier's mind
Depends on it to continually wind;
Remember those napkin-inscribed business plans
That intellect alone could not devise.

Oh - intuition - why does Man
Take such little heed of what you see.
This species that slaughters endlessly,
Simply for lack of hearing thee.

HE COMPOSES WRIT; OR, AN ODE
TO COSMIC INTELLIGENCE

It is a mystery I cannot surmise,
It still does my intellect surprise,
The manner in which my verse does pour
Leaves me in wonder - and, still more, in sacred awe.

What vistas does intuition scan,
How does it, literary jewels find?
What starry regions does it quest,
To quell young writers' unrest?

How does it, friend, in silence sing
And to aching hearts, serenity bring?
What voice does it echo, I'd call it God,
But did Nietzche not quip, 'Gott ist Tot'?

You see:
No true composer, be it of tune,
Or rhyme or writ, or verse.
Can doubt that beyond reason's chimerical ways,
Does live a resplendent voice true.

For in moments of artists' melancholy, lain
It spells Life's Truths, full plain.
And lifted beyond space-time's confines,
Such composers do the Eternal find.

I know my brethren, of creative bent
Know what is here sent,
Be Truth.
And aye,
'Tis truer still
That the Creative Mind
(Of which all men are blessed),
Verily be, the Creator's child.

WISDOM'S LAND

Egypt beckons, I hear its call -
The land of swirling sands that long ago did fall.
Where Kings and scholars once did meet,
And mathematical graces raise; what a sublime feat.
A tear is shed, when I reminisce
On her tender touch, and her empyrean kiss -
A Queen, in whose bosom I did in comfort lay,
Oh Egypt, rise again, this I pray.

DUST OF THE ANCIENTS

This science my Ancient teachers knew
And shared only with the very few,
Shall be for modern men remade as new,
So that all may partake of Divine dew.

And Man cannot conceive what lies in store
When this Ancient Science he shall restore.
That'll lead him on to empyrean heights
And ever-ascending glorious might

When on forbidden fruit he does correctly feed,
So that God himself, he may His face meet.
And at last humankind shall finally realize
Our Father's glory is beyond anything we can e'en
surmise.

EGYPT'S RISE

It comes ever so silenty
In whispered tone, and low-hushed tune
When resting, basked in reverie
And to all uncouth thoughts immune.
That maybe land where pharaohs lay
Was home of neurobiophysicists
Who knew far beyond our day
And were high-end empiricists.
And that we shall one day concede,
They knew far more than we admit,
But in conceit we do recede
When our pride does not submit.
But Aquarian spring that does now rain
Awaits the glory dawning here,
The splendours we shall see again
When Egypt's science we make clear.
In modern terminology,
Divested of mystic poesy

Confusing phenomenology
And nonsensical 'spirituality',
So Man may once more stand and gaze
At glories that are from him now hid
When past this Kali-Yuga phase,
Regain glory from which he has slid.
And aching Earth to glory restore
Her long lost pristine purity
With wisdom from the other shore.
And bless us with serenity
And yes, permit us to behold
Glories we can't yet even conceive -
Dream of things that now must be told,
Secrets that in ecstasy, we shall receive.
When bless'd with higher consciousness,
'Tis paradise, our brains shall see -
For when by its 'Sacred Science' blessed,
Forgotten Egypt's rise, shall set us all free!

THE ROYAL ART

I placed my brain up on the stand
To be chiselled in accord to Nature's plan.
All faith I put in providential hand
'Til from rooftops, I did exclaim "I can!".
I am by plasmic serpent bit,
That does my neuronal circuits knit.
And permits fine poetic writ
Until in sacred awe I sit.
And wonder at the splendor
Of Creation and the error
Of the Nation and the furor
That shall rise when in their stupor
They concede that the Lord does not
Perchance carve out this lot
For humans to just let it rot
Else Nature shall create a knot
That shall not reverse until
Man's stubborn ways are changed and his will
To live corrected and he at last stands still
To the voice of Providence screaming now from
Heaven's hill!

KUNDALINI TIDINGS

My brain oft fills with startling flow
That does at times surprise me so.
Why? This, dear friend I do not know
This certainly is not for show.
The mysteries of initiates be
They say, enshrined in secrecy
But a mystery known to Indian lore, 'Kundalini'
Yes, shall change it all.
I see a world divinely brush'd
By its kindest Diwali touch;
A race of God-Men shall embrace
Its tenets and the whole world grace.

SERPENT POWER

Friend, I do daily of my glial cells sup
An ambrosial wine that does like fine snow
Precociously, treacle from ever high up,
To once more into, my third-ventricle flow.

Physiological poesy is a strange delight,
And its root, I confess, does my own senses astound.
That Nature has destined Man for this sublimest
inner flight,
I aver to be true, and of this, stand my ground.

AURUM POTABILE

'Tis not from Man hid but in plain sight,
The Elixir to restore his might.
That supped, grants him a Cosmic view
Of life -
The secret vouchsafed,
For aeons
But, to the few.

And if mortal man
Could but partake
Of this sun-brushed
Daily renewed
Ambrosial dew,
He would
Verily,
As the phoenix, rise;
Crown-prince of Aquarius' sunrise.

IT CONSUMETH ME: AN ODE TO ALCHEMY

I am filled to the brim with a living light
That courses through my veins and becomes my
might.
What modern science says 'tis not all right
Research this liquid gold, this is my plight!

Out of invisible airs do my words spring,
And to me a fine wisdom, do they bring.
Whilst still yet a mortal I see heaven's air
And a poet's gown I now do wear.

'Tis of this power that Hermes wrote,
And his fine verse here, I now do quote
"What is above, is as below,
Raise it to heaven, and let it flow".

It has by many names been sold,
A secret that is rarely told,
Harness now what is within thee
And soar as the angels, that you see

Painted upon the finest chapel walls
Raised by the masters, when in overalls
They visioned this, and for it pitted all,
'Renaissance men' we do them call.

And Mozart, him too, he knew this art,
Its every bit and every part
His genius, nay, it was not born
And with beauty did he this world adorn.

This gift here, 'tis for us all to seize;
It is your birthright, you must not cease
To search 'til its secrets you do unfold -
Come now dear friend, be bold!

OH, ALCHEMY

Who amongst you would even dream
Of delving into the mystic stream
Of alchemical lore galore,
And dare walk through that ancient door

Into a room, blackened as night,
Mist-filled with vapour you must fight
To see, who beckons when sound strikes the ear
And alembics, vessels, potent elixirs stir.

This is the image one does frame,
When presented with this eerie name
With arcane tone, oh poor alchemy
How misunderstood you do seem to be.

If only my dear brothers here
Could see how I do hold you dear.
You have bless'd me with the highest gifts,
And to Heaven's highest regions you do me daily
lift.

So this ode for you I do compose,
So modern men may at least suppose
There is truth where e'er your tenets be
I lie not - this they shall one day see

That alchemists were not madmen, nay
But scientists of a high class, they
Mere sought in a meticulous way
To accelerate evolution's tardy pace

So man could with high consciousness stand,
And gaze, aye, maybe e'en understand
The mysteries of the sages old,
And myths that for ages have been told

Once spinal serpent he learnt to tame
And inner lion, trained himself to grasp,
So fiery dragon would not him maim
But bless him more and more, 'til he would gasp

At wonders that before him would unfold
And mysteries he would now know, still untold,
Wise words he would with pen intone
When blessed by pineal Philosopher's Stone.

Squire, these truths that I have herenow laid bare,
Make haste, put to use and be aware
(As the bard himself did quip):
There exists much above, and below
That your o'er proud science, does not even know.

THE DRAGON

A fiery dragon inside me burns
So fine-textured hormonal tincture churns;
An eletromagnetic engulfing blaze
That does confuse my startled gaze.
So I now question all thought I knew -
My assumptions, out of the window flew
When, a year ago - that be exact
Come listen here, this be a fact:
I awoke, from a sweet gentle doze;
An ever mild pleasant repose,
And showery radiance did emerge
From spinal base - now do not judge
My senses they were ever clear
And this secret, I hold very dear -
Into my cranial dome did flow
A sparkling essence, yes I know
What I say now, such fiction seems,
Please do not now plot clever teams
Who will make my fine empirical
Observation, seem hysterical,
For trained from rigid schools, I stand

And with scientific ways thus can
Elucidate the false, from fact,
I tell you - this is not an act.
And future scholars shall confirm
This experience and bring solid firm
Confirmation, to show to science lore
There is indeed much left in store
To sift through and uncover - friend
Do not be fooled by modern trend,
That fashions with material aim
Which shall soon your cerebrum maim.
And question - if I a madman be
How has this writ here, you now do see
Emerged? When barely months ago
I struggled, and now it does profusely flow --
So come join this 'applied-neuroscience' spree
So that hand-in-hand, we can inwardly fly free
And blaze new trails - oh, tis such a rush
To be blessed by Kundalini's touch!

MYSTIC'S BIOLOGY

This gentle, sweeping, pulsing flow,
Enchanting, sparkling, seething glow,
A coursing, brushing stunning show
Is guided by Hand I cannot know

With mortal mind that can't conceive
Infinity, and does not believe
In Spirit - but 'tis as if my senses deceive
So convincingly; surely it can't these Truths
receive!

And though I myself a sceptic be,
This evidence suffices for me
That there does exist so much it seems,
Beyond the things that I do see.

This 'secret fire' has my skull reshap'd
And my entire visage remade:
And whenever I sup from that sweet golden lake
It does, me, swift, to Heaven take!

BUDDHA THE NEUROSCIENTIST

I find it most astounding see,
That the Lord in the body be;
An electric ferment that does bless
With ever higher consciousness.
Siddartha, friends, it seems to me,
Possessed a neuroscience degree,
Which he applied to his sprouting mind
'Til' his hemispheres intertwin'd.
Low-latence gripped, his startled gaze,
Witnessed a divine lit blaze.
Samadhi dripped, a soul now free,
He reposed b'neath neuronal Bodhi tree.
So to religious pomp, I bite my thumb,
And laugh until my sides are numb -
Aye - science, it seems shall win the day,
For highly empirical, is the Middle Way.

ALTRUISM TRUE

Altruism is all well and good
Once it is full understood,
That acting 'pon the desire to others help
Begins, first, with a harmonious self.

OH MAN!

Oh mankind mend thy wretched ways
That'll lead you onto tarnished days,
Of suffer'ngs, ever bleak and dark
When you do on this doomed route embark.

Why must a fellow brother sing
In lyric, so your ears do ring.
You've silenced intuition's bell
'Til in spiritual darkness you now do dwell.

And quip not, that was I say is false,
For one minute, dear friend, do sit and pause.
Observe the terrain, now on earth lain
And millions that have now been slain

Since from primordial heap we sprang
(To which we should our Father thank) -
We've done injustice to evolution's cause
And yet still do ourselves applaud

Whilst angels, in the starry sky
Do mock, nay, shake their heads and cry,
That God's own children, once so tame
Have wrough such havoc, it does his Great Name
shame.

THE VENUS PROJECT

I am humbled by Jacque Fresco's plan
Of a splendidly clad God-Man's land
That shall know simple common-sense
And free our world of the pestilence
That now corrupts its high ideals
And stinks of rotten corrupt deals
Of selfish bankers who are bent,
On spending what to them is lent
On piffle, dark, shameful pursuits,
And man-made exploitaton suits;
Whilst their brethren torn in other lands
They leave to sordid dictators' hands.
And not for a second reckon how it
Feels, when by cold poverty hit
To know naught but harsh frozen times
And for a lifetime beg of simple dimes
To feed your bone-starved children
But with nothing - and in guilty concern
You bring a bullet to the head
For anguish filled, you do still dread
The look of starving partner's face
Who now bereft of all her grace
Can't figure how her husband talks
And his ever frequent lonely walks
Cannot his impov'rished household feed
When those he knows in dire need
Are shipwrecked; has the Lord decreed
The black race, shall never be freed?!
So Fresco - my hat I off do take
As you push for our world to remake;
May your dream sent from up on high
See light of day in this Earthly sky.

Heavy questions did weigh on his mind,
Answers for which
he could not find.
A nation finding itself hard-wrought
For freedom, it had for decades fought.
Yet in it, the Negro-man did
Find himself, full-chained then, and enslaved
Despite the nation's decree
That all men, under God be equal,
And justly, therefore, are free.
Still, there was little that Lincoln
He could do,
The Nation's cold ways stood hard to budge,
For the men from South,
And the North
Both
Did nought, but the negro, judge.

And here with modern perspective blest,
We simply with his problems wrest
And though its solution now so simple stands,
Its full complexity we cannot test.

What can a man do
Who loves his kin,
And slave-men he sees as brothers too?
Must he from the former's opinions abscond
Thustly destroying the nation's bond?
What can he say when he knows their ways,
Do their own Constitution betray?

Must he their foolishness display
Of their ways, stage a play?
And pray tell, this; how does he prove,
That all men equal be?
When in that dark time, only men of their own skin
Did they such a light see.

Such was the mental load,
That Lincoln himself
Did nearly fail to hold.
And yet tried, as best he could,
Despite how the climate stood
To do as true-men should.

And thus, his memorial today stands,
To grace Washington bright
Our memory of a man,
Led by Providence's hand
To lead America on, to'ard the Light.

And may this Nation in our day
Remember its predestined Way.
May it ne'er forget, and understand
The wisdom for which America was meant to stand,
Let it pave the broad way to Harmony,
And never again from the Truth sway.

THE FOURTH COMMANDMENT

That Man does not Sabbath Day properly keep,
Does make this young brother, sorrowfully weep.
For steeped in blind ignorance, mankind does not
know
The spirit-from-letter that from prophets did flow.

That Adam and Eve in the Garden did sin,
To forfeit all glories they were destined to win
Should indeed make even the most shallow of
minds,
Realise how severely the human race has gone
blind.

For it cannot see 'twas evolution's strict law
We broke, and are now trapped in the claw
Of mortal flesh fetters; from Paradise lost,
Yet still in conceit, do of our own 'glory' boast,

Not knowing, the Grand Architect has in turn
Devised cosmic laws, to which mankind must stay
true.
And the 'mystical' vision borne of Heavenly dew
By free-will, he decrees we must now choose to
earn:

Now in truth, what does mark of a true Israelite
Is one whose own body daily fills with Light;
The 'chosen ones', are not picked by birth,
But those who by self-effort have now shown their
worth.

To witness sweet glories they cannot define
When the strait and narrow way, they finally find -
These are the Leviathans who'll serenity see
When cloaked in their Father's rawest majesty.

And God himself, nay, not so 'strait-laced' he be,
'Tis in fact your own glory, he wishes to see.
So from now, set aside this most holy of days
To internalise the ageless tenets of Evolution's True
Way.

And when you do daily of fine chrism partake
Sup deeply the waters of that liquid-fire lake!
And Veritas, she who all humankind seeks,
You'll behold when gazing from Mount Sinai's
high peak!

WHY WAIT

Why wait until consultancy
To walk with bold authority,
You prance ever uncandidly
'Til friends of thee, ashamed all be.

Why wait until the eve of death
To worry how it stands, your health -
You think it will forever last?
When poorest dice you now do cast.

Why wait until you lose the prize
'Til sense again retrains your eyes.
A love sweet as fine gold is worth
You let go for much lesser dearth.

Must humans' lack of foresight be
So shameful, for we do not see
How carelessly and thoughtlessly
We cast our gifts into the sea.

And still we pray for boon of wealth,
And mourn when we do lose this pelf.
Man, this world you see mirrors your flaws
And you yourself bring on your wars.

For your own sake, remake your ways,
They are so numbered, now, your days -
In not too long you shall all see
The lesson Heav'n has in store for thee.

GNOTHI SEAUTON

Whene'er a soul be unmasked, lain,
Its true beauty does, without words, stand plain,
Thus, effortlessly arrives that wish
To be loved, honoured, and cheris'd.
So to mortal man who does strive for pelf
Say I, "brother, seek ye first, to 'Know Thyself".
For all the gold you now so fervent seek
Is to be found within Thineself.

OH, CAPITALIST

Man too easily
Forgets that his impulse to be rich,
Exists
So he may his,
And the lives of others
Enrich.
And ego-trapped,
Forfeits his lofty dreams
For the - oh so
Ephemeral - means.

LOST

For each of us shall come a time
When sick of every childish crime,
We'll leave behind the toys of youth
To begin the ardent pursuit of Truth.

In manner that we do not know,
This impulse here will itself show.
Our incessant minds then will not rest
'Til we realize that this is a test

Of free-will gained, and now near lost,
When Man permits to be the host
Of petty urges and denies
The Lord entry into their very lives.

But if 'tis happiness Mankind truly seeks,
It must reorganize a civil 'order' that reeks
Of sheer anarchy, so it may align
In harmony, with Evolution's plan.

So that perchance, on a future day,
It'll taste the light of serenity's rays;
Sun-clothed; in samadhi blissened trance,
Divine sparks, at last with God, will dance.

THE SLAVE

What use is the world's mightiest Wealth
And an impregnable mental stealth,
When all the while you destroy your health
And of Love, leave your family in dearth?

WE BLIND MEN

This mortal Man
Cloaked in ephemeral delights
Strives
With all the might at his command
To summon a reason for his existence.

Little does he know
Of the nucleus of his being,
The ground of Him-Self
That surpasses (one-thousand
Fold) - all the pleasures that he sees.
And all this - merely by being Still.

Dimmed - is his consciousness;
His awareness asleep.
When a blind man tells you that there is no Light.
Should he be believed -
Shall you his reasoning keep?

But still you do -
For the allure of the transient
Is strong.

We are -
Immortals in pain
Enchained.
Slaves.

PART II

DESPAIR

With the merciless destruction of former psychological constructs of reality, one is flung into a veritable existential abyss, where there is no anchor to be found. There is only hopelessness, darkness, desperation and despair. Love has forsaken us. Why would it do such a thing? What are we to do now? We weep with a deep inner sobbing, for what feels like an eternity. The 'dark night of the soul' is upon us. Help. Please. Anyone. Anything. Please.

OH, WOMAN!

Oh woman!

Maker of dreams and maker of streams -
Of tears.
No man can live up to your
Phantasies.
Not even the poet.

Oh woman!
In your flight of ideas you concoct
the perfect world
Of unattainable delights;
Dreams yet unrealised that no mortal
man can satisfy.

Oh woman!
How you thirst for love
But receive it not.
For adulation
But accept it not.

Oh woman;
Even with Zeus, unsatisfied.

Oh woman - woe to thee, oh enigma
Of all ages.
We pine for thee, and cry for thee
And when with thee
Plead, "make haste woman...and depart from me".

Oh woman;
Poets lament that thoughts of thee,
run for pages;
Their blackened tears in published writ.

Oh woman: mystery of all ages.
What is it thouest want?
See - you yourselves knowest it not.

Oh woman, oh woman.
Oh woman indeed.

HABIBTI

Oh:
You heavenly Pearl of Arab
Springs.
Of whose virtues I have preached!
Whose skin glows as the moonlight,
And possesses that golden dove-touch.

For aeons I have sought thee,
For ages, pined for thee.
And now -
When my soul does you see
When at last I am found
(When once I was lost)
Your Spirit knows me not.

Woe, to this anguish
That embraces me.
But it must,
For in its embrace I find solace.
For wherever my thoughts fly with you -
Is Paradise.
So let me suffer
Nostalgia
For millennia.
If it be for you, my love,
To anything, I shall gladly concede.

Habibti;
I breathe for thee.
Exist for thee
And long for thee.
Insh'Allah, the stars shall conspire
For us.
For our love.
For this Truth.
My dearest - my soul does you already clearly see.
And it prays,
That one day,
You too, shall see
Me.

GOODBYE MY LOVER

Oh lover, for aeons for you
I did pine,
My mind
Tormented.

Aged 13,
One moon's gaze
Set this heart ablaze
Lit.
Sublime.
Empyrean.
Heavenly -
Oh! The fleeting wonders of ephemeral delight.

But in my heartbreak you watched me
But did nothing.
And silently, I wept.
Alone;
A loner
Lonesome.
Reclused,
The meandering tears golden,
But parched
By this jilted love.

Or was it -
What was it you hid?
Questions unanswered.
My heart aflame seeking deliverance
But remembrance,
Keeping me
Imprisoned.

You loved - or did you?
I can only
But wonder,
When I stood alone.
In my pain, was I carried
By you, oh 'lover' -
Were my anguished tears in vain?
For they sought the silk touch of
Your high Grace
That modern science calls,
Fingers;
Their presence, a teardrop's relief.

Where was your kindness
Oh lover?
With it, you could have
Anointed this mind
With the balm of its nectarian touch
Granting serenity,
Peace
Of mind
To this tortured,
And seemingly vanquished
Esprit.

Lover:

Perchance, someday we'll meet
And sit,
And poetic eloquence shall be our dish;

God's fulfilment of Cupidon's wish.

But my heart it still sorely weeps.
So my lover -
From your radiance must my face be hid
I shall happ'ly survive
Without the sustenance of your love.
Or a love I sought,
And found not.

Goodbye, dear lover -

Farewell.

If I told you what it is I felt,
How you caused my heart to melt,
I fear I'd cause your own feelings to sway
And swift,
Frighten you away.

So I vow to forever here, in silence lay,
My tempted lips, restrain from giving way.
And as I would with
A glorious distant star:
'Til Eternity - admire you.
But only
From afar.

TELL ME FRIEND

Can aching hearts ever again sing
As in times that did sweetest joy bring.
What Titan might can e'en restore
Wisdom, brought from the other shore?

Young poets with high wisdom graced
When their heart, pure-love interlaced
Supped, of Heaven's empyrean stream,
Penned lyrics, as if in a dream.

When mystic stream did in abundance flow,
'Til pineal lamp, as a solar orb would glow.
Love-vested, heart brim-filled with pride,
When 'pon Heavenly clouds, their soul did glide.

Tell me friend:

Can aching hearts hearts ever again sing,
As in times that did sweetest joy bring.
Can aching hearts, once more taste love's high note,
And live true again, the bliss of which they wrote?

WHEN

I cared far more than you may know,
Far more than I cared to show.
Far more even, than you knew then,
But I did wonder -
When?

When would I speak, and voice my heart,
Would I slowly suffer, and never start
A river, whose stream had begun to flow -
A heart softly aglow?

When would I tell you how I felt,
Where my soul it truly dwelt?
To my friends, I would, of you oft tell,
And daily in prayer, wish you well.

When would you know that 'twas your brain,
In which, my spirit'd lain?
And solace found in your sharp wit,
Much peace, when we again did meet.

A mind of brilliance
Surpassing Nirvana's instance.
'Tis how
Much I cherished it,
Your cerebral power.
Oh and
You! - A blossoming
Soular flower.

But in anger's grip,
I did fast quip
Words, that in reminisce
Seem ill-flung.
Oh - and how my heart
You
Now, does so painfully miss.

BIPOLAR

When she holds you as a God
In her eyes - know that
Soon
As a demon you shall seem.
Hellish.
Where before she saw light -
She shall recognise only darkness,
Where there was joy -
Only despair.
You shall despair
And be the despair;
Her despair.

Know this:

Where before she held you
In her
Eyes
As a being of Light.
You shall soon extinguished be. For
Who she idolises,
She soon demonises.

It settles,
What rises.
All falls,
That soars.

'Tis sad, I know. It
Brings well-springs to my eyes
Too -
But in such a manner, my friend, seems to
function
That capricious bipolar mind.

BADASS

Troubled minds
Seek troubled waters,
For where else can they swim?
When heartbreaks' remnants
Create caprice,
And free love
On a whim.

ON MISSING YOU

Though it is by Her that he is writ-employed,
Must the Muse also the Poet destroy?
In ethereal realms he dwells, when through Her
An afflatus is sent,
Then by Her absence, he is verily bleak-rent.

SHADES OF BLACK

Devoutly strung on high soul's peak
It is mere love we seek.
E'en though in weakness to receive
It, 'tis something we can't conceive.

And battered by life's acid rains
That do o'er rack our brains.
Meek souls, first lambs, now
By life entrained
'Til 'tis fierce wolves the world sees.

But, ye, come now
And ponder how
'Tis tarnished past that has,
Moulded kind souls, over again
And our once sweet spirits drain'd.

So from affection's door
(Without which
Even the wealthiest men remain poor)
We self-bar ourselves
And in our pain,
Take to emotion's cane.

And with this dry writ
I do here sit
And ponder some more that,
Despite treasures which
Stand by me lain
I still daily over feign.

For my heart still weeps,
For love-pure yearns,
That it may into my soul seep;
Friend remember that
E'en chiseled hearts, of 50 grades
Are possessed of still sweeter shades.

And who cares to see,
May set us free
From this imposed love-exile.
I ask of thee, nay, I dare thee:
Come - and ye shall see our true smile...

HER SIN

In loving others,
It does seem
He did her feelings hurt.
But the blame fell on her part
For
She tried to wrest,
And possess a poet's heart.

RETROSPECTOSCOPE

The poets say love is so blind,
It leaves good common sense behind.
But let us remember full well
We all have many such tales to tell.

'Tis easy when in restrospect
To decipher when things were so suspect;
Hindsight 'tis a blessing that shows us how
Silly we can be in the now.

DREAMS

In flowery rhetoric
Do poets frequently quip,
That does naught but shred their already
anguished hearts.

In dreams alone
Does the true Poet dwell;
An eternal blessing
Yet a curse indeed

DIVINE DISCONTENT

Where is she?
Does she e'en exist,
Hid behind mortal mists?
Where is she
For whom my heart doth pine
Will I her,
Ever find?
What if talk of
One's other half
Is merely but a myth.
What then
Shall the earth's Poets, drive;
What for, then
Shall we strive?

MY PILGRIMAGE

Sweet girl, what would I not have given
To have your love received?
I sit in pain, as I do you miss,
Yet you did my feelings dismiss.

What mountains must a man surmount
To prove that from this fount -
His heart -
Does flow an Infinite stream
Of love
That can daily grow,
And transmute life into a wondrous dream.

For aeons I did dwell on thee
How could you not this see?
I made my feelings ever plain
Despite what you did claim.
I sat and dreamt
Of where you dwelt,
Of how to you appease
I dreamt of peace
In reverie,
And saw you
As my Queen.

And perchance brash,
Through trembling lips
I did it all confess.
What had for ages
In silence lain -
I did bravely profess.

And it now make sense
What Yeats did warn -
That one should on young hearts
Softly tread -
For it manifested
What I did dread,
Leaving my meek spirit near-dead.

But mortal pride
You know, hard dies
For self-esteem must be retained.
And so I swiftly, did respond
To my manhood reclaim.

But
Must dignity regained
Always mean lovers' loss,
When not requited.
Must hellish pangs
For ever be the lot
Of those who
But, seek true love?

I knelt for thee,
Your name my prayer -
Your footsteps my soul's true song;
Their Path my destiny.
My hymns, soul-sung, shall never age,
You were my Pilgrimage.

PATIENT'S SON

I saw my mother bed-rid
And in body ache;
It tasked her
Even, to mildly wake.
What terror fills the mind of a startled
physician-son
Who gasps in awe at what has transpired thus?
What questions does he pose of this mortal run,
Whose light is threatened by the hour of life's
Midday sun?
'Tis not with joyful wail with which he does
exclaim,
Nor does he find fault in others, or swift lay blame.
But rather his inquisitive mind, does inquire, all
the more,
Of what else this ephemeral life does have in store.

And from this anguished, existential pose
Did blossom forth, a most exquisite Rose
Of wisdom flowing, from intuition's fount
That taught me love and where it should be found:

Love 'tis not a ray preserved for other suns,
Nor the privy of reclused and blindly faithful nuns.
But rather, it does within all men and women lie
If they merely bothered to
Into the Inner World, pry.

The lessons from that serene song of harmony
Did teach me that Love is never beyond our reach,
But rather in the bosom of each
And every mortal lies;
It is that glint seen in every human eye.

And from that wisdom, of which I did partake
I learnt I must none ever for granted take.
But rather, each second, hour, day and Spring
Seek, into a moment truly joyous to make
Whence mortals and immortals - both - in unison,
can sing.
'Til sublime ethers, do from the Heavens ring
To make life a sweet play forever more.

GUARDIAN ANGEL

Where's my guardian angel
When I do lie here unwell?
A mother's Love
In such
Times
Does seem the kindest touch.

Where's my guardian angel
When self-pity drips
From my brow.

A mother's hand,
A nurse's brush -
She somehow seems to know how.

When illness struck
Several years yore
E'en before wisdom had to me come,
Sweet mother's way
Did gently sway
Me back to wellness' way.

And that's my guardian angel
Who rescues me from illness' shore
E'en through life's twists
And feuds and trials
Still,
She's remained a golden guardian angel
Now
And shall Forever-more

OH, HOSPITAL

Too much sadness,
Too much death,
Too much abject loneliness.
Too much pondering upon when there I'll be
Reflecting upon my life,
and where it all went.
Too much suff'ring
'Tis what I see
Augmenting the voice of my own pleas
That still incessantly rings,
Wondering on this, and what it all means.
A wish to mitigate the pain,
A prayer to soften the inner ache.
For now, grit my teeth
And feign a grin,
Labour'ing toward that day I shall at last be free.

Unruly wards where chaos does reign,
And physicians must a supreme strength feign,
Having laboured-long, 'til night meets day
And do for respite pray.

Where senses are full overwhelmed,
Where one does beg for it to quell.
Restless esprits that do in Hades dwell
To quench others' agony.

This sight of death, it does turn men
Into Philosophers, for it swift brings
That 'Shortness of Life' of which Seneca sings,
Into Reality.

SENIOR BE KIND; OR, A JUNIOR DOCTOR SPEAKS

If medicine the practice of Compassion be
Tell me - why do I so oft see?
Some seniors who self-righteous feel
And the limelight, do fight to steal.

If this truly Royal Art
Be Heaven's start,
In part-relieving this ill world's ache,
Why then do some physicians seem to
Delight
In watching their younger brethren break?

Must kindness so selective be,
Bondaged, what should righty be free?
Have you ever, friend,
Seen the sun's rays basked
Upon a single, cornered scene?

Must love that that should always radiate
Suddenly towards colleagues abate.
'You useless, senseless idiotic fool'
Through their eyes they state,
Making you feel worse e'en,
Than a mere tool.

This paradox, its seems, is oft enacted
By those who (by now) should have learned
That respect, honour, trust and love
Be high-gifts, and they are earned.

Not by strutting around,
In hand-crafted suits
And expensive shoes to boot.
Yet
Leaving on wards a horrid stench,
A sense of over-importance that
To others truly reeks.

Not by judging, and casting an evil eye
On other staff,
'Do they not know who the hell I be?'
A pathetic show
That leaves one truly pitiful
Towards those hosting the play;
(For their thoughts one can almost see).

Nor by voicing strings of endless harangue,
With incessant wails that do frustrate.
Tactically dealt humiliations
That leaves juniors wishing to themselves end.

I shall swiftly
Now rest my case,
And simply now here request:
Stressed seniors, forget not
That Compassion, must be so deeply imbued,
That it does
Even one's junior colleagues include.

PATIENTS' ACHE

Through my swift-penned mystical muse
(Borne of life's perspectives perused),
I loudly ponder what beyond us, stands lain
And why life does oft seem plain.

Must frolick and fun be
The simple plan,
Of an 80 year life-span.
Must slaving for another man's luxurious car,
Be where we set the bar?

Must fleeting joys
Aided by liquor-tinctures, be the perpetual boon
Of the mortal man's domain.
Must reckless, 'fun' debauchery
Forever be, the plan of another day.

And in this pensive fit I do recall
My elderly patients, seen.
Who to tumultuous mental lands have been
And now in ill health be.
And oftentimes do contemplate
What it must be like to roam,
Into their experiences rich-filled,
Relive their former trips to Rome.

What wisdom would these souls impart,
With what lessons would they start?
What would they think of my many wrongs;
Of when I failed to hear life's songs?

What would they say -with wit unmatched -
To my burning questions match?
I am not fooled, for though they frail they be,
Their eyes do with wisdom gleam.

And what of those to whom death nears
What make they of their fears?
No doubt this life has spared them not,
And now Death is to be their lot.

What fills the mind of an ailing man
When told he is soon to die?
By what terror must his soul be gripped,
Of his impending Hades trip.
Perchance 'tis majestic song that does his soul fill-
And he does silenty rejoice.
But nay - I have not yet a patient seen
Who has faced death with hopeful voice.

And so daily, I do reflect;
From the senses withdraw.
Attempt to orchestrate and plan,
A meaningful life draw.
But oft it fails me
And I cannot see
The purpose if this mad life-spree.
And dark clouds thence do hijack joy's light
Leaving me stark, in fright.

Seeing patients' ache
Aye - it does startle,
From mere vulgar ambition wakes.
Forcing a man to - with renewed mind - consider
What He shall, of this short-life make.

4AM

Tis past the midnight-hour
Yet I toss and turn and find
I cannot rest,
And pray my darling's soothing kiss
Will free me from this unrest.
For it seems the Poets' penchant that
When we do supine lay,
Inwardly we ruminate
And contemplate
This life's confusing play.

TEARDROP

Drowned in this life's transient sea
That passes fleetingly,
Poets oft to the Heavens scorn
And question why e'er they were born.
For questions that unanswered be
Do these meek souls torment.
Why existence does so treacherously
Treat us, and why are we here sent,
Fighting the desire to now-here abscond;
Cut loose this mortal bond.
The poet's life, 'tis not all a song
So life - please spare us all this wrong.

AMBITION'S SIN

How young men do quest to be rich
But in their zeal forget,
The wealth with which this life does them vest
Is intended to, the Inner Life enrich.

Yet these ego-driven tyrants spend
A half-part, still, and more
Of their jewelled-time, in a hot-pursuit of pelf,
That does toward sure destruction tend.

Only - it seems - to be denied
That which they in fact first sought,
Unbridled propelled, they do lose sight
Of the Beauty for which they once fought.

DELUSIONALS

Too many mortal men it seems
Do shift their dreams
For ease.
For comfort
And some mental rest
When they are by life's torrents spent.

So how can we here even know
Who has fulfilled their dream -
This planet where all is a show;
A mirage that is nought but steam.

MY SONG

We poets be
Cursed with hearts that too easily bruise,
And with minds that can of our pain muse.
"Ich vermisse dich",
I did last week speak
When this fire had reached its peak.
I've longed - and longed, again
'Til, I can no more long.
And this early morn',
I do now mourn
You,
For truly you have been
My song.

OF HEAVEN DREAM

Though it be our own Illusions that make our
Poor hearts scream,
What Poet, does not of Heaven dream?

GOLGOTHA

I am
Torn by this fatalistic mental stream
That renders this life
But a dream.
And when into me it peeks,
'Tis then, high-wisdom that I do seek,
Where in my secret enclave
I do a brighter future pave.
Must all initiates
Such anguish, on
This mortal plane taste?

A YOUNG POET'S LAMENT

For a man who worships True Love so,
Why does True Love ne'er smile down on me.
Perchance it has been by the Heavens fated
That's its Immortal rays I must not see.
For sat here it seems,
That thing for which all poets pine,
The stars have decreed I must never find.

And whene'er it seems I do, only a dose minute
Is upon my parched tongue vouchsafed,
'Til I plead the gods for their sweet Ambrosia;
That Elixir that is sweet Love's touch.
Aye - the poets' gift, 'tis the poets' curse;
It bruises
And it does nurse.
Oh!
What Mystery does bequeath with so large a love-
vessel -
Then cruelly debars one from the Essence that
does it fill.

HUMAN NATURE; OR, MY MOST PAINFUL LESSON YET

It praises the dead,
Curses the living,
Leaving deep wounds in its stead.
What use is a funeral rhapsody
When a living friend's virtues it never can see.
And grief-stricken mortals, then do pine
'Til fulgent tears
From their eyes do shine.
Would you
Such kindness, friend have shown
If yours had been blessed with many more years?
They abandon who live,
To dead men grieve
Until those they left
E'en, they pass too.
Then once more, new tears do overflow -
'Oh lost friend, I loved you so!'
Must Death forever be what
Jogs our sense;
Can we not, before its arrival, Love?
It aches - for I too have oft, likewise sinned.
Our Human Nature - it baffles me so.

ME

Will I be more noble in this life than the last,
Will I still hold grudges, or let go of the past.
Will I love greatly, and yet even greater still
When others have scorned me

And

From it garnered their fill?

Will I show kindness, when I have been spurned,
Show temperance when it is for revenge that I
yearn,
Will patience adorn me, though still restless I am,
Will I hold my tongue, even though correct I may
be?

What will I be, with this short-life here blessed
Will it by a sweet robe be luxuriously dressed?
Will kind raiment be the fruits of my labour on
Earth,
Will my descendants mourn, on the eve of my
death?

What will I be;
What will my mortal life see?
What will I be?
I will only be
Me.

PENSIVE

This black poet doth contemplate
How Heaven has decreed,
That certain men by verse would state
The truth of Beauty's creed.
For numb struck by their muse they shall
Their wit by pen return,
In high sounding names such as 'Parzival',
And sweet 'Odes to Grecian Urns'.
Yet still somehow in their honey-prose
Find the time to lament,
Such that upon reflection one may suppose
Their Fate is Hades-sent.

THE MODERN POET

The modern poet
He doth ache,
More than his brethren of former ages.
And numerous mental pages
He does fill
When his consciousness stands still.
Many sentiments he does
Under his inner bushel hide,
Perchance someone shall one day attempt
To his inner treasure find.
But
'Til then Philosophy
Shall his daily solace be
Until he does,
A heavenly place
See.

THE POETS' FATE

Our dreams belong beyond this state
In regions where the gods do ambrosia taste,
Luscious planes that
Shall never here manifest;
This is the Poet's fate.

To dream and ne'er have them fulfilled.
And vision, yet have it all sullied,
And as Sisyphus,
Push onward - yet still
Lament -
This wretched Poet's fate.

Adorned inward, with resplendent light,
That outward-sight shall never match.
Do wipe these tears,
Understand our plight;
We bare
The Poets' fate.

ALL IS FAIR

It has been said
That all acts pertaining to Love and War, be fair.
'Til e'en Life's Great Pearl is used as a trap
To unsuspecting souls ensnare.
Where are those who truly can
Of their soul's essence give.
Who can, despite their fear-racked brains, take
that risk
To, truly Live.
Man's capricious ways
Make for somber days
And yet still he does lament.
I do question the intellect,
That renders life derelict.

NAIVETY'S CHILD

How oft do poets in anger speak,
These lovers nowadays known as weak?
Well - how oft does this wretched life seek
To wreck us, 'til shipwrecked we reek?

Of fumigating angered breath -
Show fury, so few dare to tread
Into our lives, 'til alone we find
We are and our damage, cannot unwind.

How naive this young squire has been:
What transpired, he should have seen
In advance, and prevented with intellect -
Aye, he shall more wisely now select.

And more dispassionate shall he be
His fervent heart, he'll tame now see,
This life was not for us poets made;
Who it does bitterly curse, with lonesome
serenade.

RUSSIAN ROULETTE

Must mortal men deeply suffer so,
Brought to points where they do feel so low
They seek for greener lands to go
So they can nature's sweet joys know.

Must fate tease gentle poets so
And twist our hearts all high and low,
'Til we long from this world to go
And not one man do we wish to know.

If this be true, please tell me so
And your volumed voice, do keep it low
Whilst you lend me sweet reasons not to go -
My veiled thoughts here, you now do know.

WHAT IS LIFE?

What trickery has mortal Man
Express'd to be as Sisyphus bound.
With ailing back, strives He onward
Yet, with no end to be found.

LITTLE JOHN

Before I'd ventured so fearlessly bold,
To love -
I wish I had been told,
That the world in which we mortals dwell,
Is oft spiteful, and cold.

Perhaps such wisdom would have spared
Me the ache of knowing she did not care.
Who knows how far I would now be,
If her steps I had foreseen.

A heartbreak that leaves a young man bleak
Is not what I did Seek.
So now: I find solace in my poetic writ,
By which I shall never be bit.

TIRED

It seems
I've been working all my life
With such little time to rest.
Toiling all my life,
Striving to be 'the best'
Taking no time to glance
Or as a bubbling spirit prance.

UNDREAMING

I remember what it felt like
To have dreams;
To pine, and rise
And dream again
Of days you would in your visions see.

I have none.
My dreams are gone.

Stolen, it seems, by the ephemeral nature of joys on earth,
Impermanence, their being.

Where are they - the flowers of my youth.
Where is it?
The sun of those childhood days.

I slumber in the tears of Autumn's dew.
And awaken to the Wintery cold;
This purgatory,
Is my abode.

Perchance life will bless me with a glint of Spring.
Or Summer's rays may soon
My now hardened face, grace.

Until then
It is me.
And dead leaves.
And snow.

NUDE

Why must poets' profundity,
This trail of mystic air,
Be matched by such melancholy;
This life - it be not fair.

In sorrow's musing they do stand,
As if it were decreed.
Quip lyrics few men understand,
When sat on high Jove's steed.

These mortal dreamers, gifted here,
Still daily feel accursed.
They mere long the love of another near
Whence their fragile souls, may at last be nursed.

A POET SPENT

Clothe me in your finest vesture
So I may rest on azure sea.
Bless me with a pleasant gesture,
Your sweetest tender reverie.

Keep me in your silken arms,
Whence strength you have may be lent as mine.
Soothe me with your starry balms,
So I may on your ambrosia dine.

Father-God do heed my call
A son in need so desperate be.
Why is it, I gave my all
Yet only darkness, I now can see?

On your marvel, Earth I sit,
I consecrated, did as I was sent.
Yet now find myself, in this narrow pit;
Your young son Lord - a poet spent.

THE SECOND BIRTH

Goodbye fine world, goodbye:
I leave now with a solemn sigh -
To dwell in the land of the sky,
And to dance in the fields up high.

Goodbye fine world, goodbye -
For me, you must not cry
When to you I do say 'bye, bye',
Shed not a tear, this you must try.

Sweet world, thou hath been so dear
At all the times when I did fear.
But goodbye, fine world, goodbye -
I love thee, but cannot lie

That there was once a time, when I laid home,
crying,
Although to some it all seems so trifling.
And I did, my friends, bare such suffering
That 'tis was rare, to see me e'en smiling.

Friends do jump in glee when I do tell
Of my poesy, they oft do yell,
"Come now John, let us hear a verse
Of your joyful work, and make it terse!"

But do they know of a poet's lows
And how he pains from his so many blows
I tell thee truly, only God knows,
For men lose their heart in life's transient shadows.

In truth, poets be not 'all high'
But their work it seems, is to try
To share, their feelings so deep,
So in spite of all troubles, their brethren may sleep.

'Tis slings and arrows, we bare
And our story we readily share.
For our love for thee be as free,
As the sun that you do daily see.

Goodbye fine world, goodbye -
I oftentimes, do wonder why
I am with this melancholy cursed,
When all I long for, is to be nursed.

Hear my song, oh my dear friend,
Sup its wisdom so that you may mend
Your heart at times of any dis-ease
And smile for me, oh do this please.

Goodbye fine world, goodbye -
Hear my last verse and cherish my breath.
Goodbye, fine world goodbye -
I shall be with thee, even in 'death'.

PART III

HOPE!

We deeply take in what shall be our last breath when all of a sudden, we notice the faintest light ahead. The shadow it dimly casts makes us aware that we are in a tunnel and that there is indeed a direction to be followed, even in this wretched, seemingly directionless land of Hades. "There was in fact meaning to all of this", it reassuringly dawns on us. Life is not a waste after all! Exhausted, we drag our aching legs and with heavy outstretched arms, make our way towards the flicker. "Hope.. hope...hope", we chant to the cadence of a new uplifting mantrum.

MY ATMAN

Perchance I'll find my Dharmic path
And this incessant ache will ease.
I pray that through this Royal Art,
I'll find Nirvanic release.

For now my Atman, softly
Bids me to higher ascend.
And its sweet message - Heaven sent -
I do cherish and tend.

SPIRITUAL WARRIOR

The fighter's spirit inside me burns
Incessant; in champion's high-flight yearns
To reach, Paradise's star-brushed Peak.

Defiant.

It shall forever seek,
And find.

WHERE THERE'S A WILL

Friend, where there's a will, there always is a way
Prance and dance now, yes - be ever gay.
For when you do, with great ambition dress,
Life will you, with purest bounty bless.

But ambition, 'tis not measured merely by the
scholar's cloak,
Nor by the height of the mightiest ancient oak.
Man must not, forfeit his life for pelf
Nor for glories, adorned for his own self.

'Tis balance here we must always seek -
Look - the Ancient spelt it upon Cheop's peak!
Think wisely, of the future day:
Friend, where there's a will - there always is a way.

BEAUTY; OR, THE CURSE

Born high, was she on beauty's steed
In a world where such is rare.
No single man did she ever need,
For with her, none could compare.

By Heaven graced, this heavenly lass
Did mortal heads daily turn.
Such karmic wealth it seemed she had amass'd,
For all hearts did for her yearn.

But secretly this beautious face
Did to Heaven nighty gaze,
And prayed perchance, a knight may come
And give her true love, his sum.

Oh, how little did other green-faced girls
Who did this maiden spite,
Know that though donned in Venusian pearls,
True love was beyond her sight.

For mortal men cannot seem to see
The sweet spark of Heaven's decree.
Beauty skin deep, and deeper still
It cares not for, and the human spirit therefore
kills.

So wide-eyed glazed, sun-brushed angels
Who from Heaven, are down here sent.
Seek love, not favours, yea, truth not pelf,
E'en if it must be lent.

And to my sisters, this here note
To you, I dedicate:
To yourselves must you always remain true -
And at last, love true shall be your fate.

CHRYSALIS

Entombed in matter's coarsest drabs
I sought for comfort's resting nest,
For sweet repose and pleasant rest,
Away from fear's incessant grabs
Towards my conscience ever meek
And my condition never sweet;
Self-pity in sand-sunken feet -
A frail condition, ever weak.
Such moments now so trivial seem,
For I can my own self forgive,
And sweet love in abundance give
To others, e'en in this 'Maya' dream.
For sweetest love's divinest rays
Have here, my tender wounds redressed,
In such gentle manner, I do feel blessed
And dream onward of splendid days.
That will this charcoaled life now fill
With beauteous joys of heaven's stock -
Aye - I myself will one day mock
My folly, when my world stood still.
For now-here I do weave myself
(From finest thread of Heaven's love
Prepared by God's divinest dove)
A chrysalis for my own Self.
And soon shall as a new man rise:
Reformed, transformed and morals high.
With blossomed wings divinely fly
Where heaven's clouds shall be my prize!

ILLUMINATION

In late-night I do here so pensive sit
And ponder upon tremulous hardships wrought -
Those days of neuronal shipwrecked fit,
The battles I have so arduous fought.

So oft, I feel no wiser still -
It seems, fate here and cupid too,
Sat high, on Heaven's comic frill
Take joy in gazing upon this human zoo.

Why these harsh lessons in which we do so oft
partake,
What purpose is it, they do us serve?
If man must err, before he learns,
Why is it his spirit so desperate yearns

For more - and more still, if there is no goal?
Does God sit there, to mere cajole
Mere mortals, 'til they do sweat in vain
And scorn Heaven, when they do lose their vein.

And my verse, 'tis oft confusing writ
That flows when I am by anguish bit.
But I do pray, we shall all see a wiser day
Whence Olympia'll gloss us with its celestial ray.

And my heartfelt wish goes to my earthly kin,
My brethren yes, though we all do sin,
Our necks shall one day in Heaven rise,
Sun-brushed by Illumination's new sunrise.

PRODIGAL

In frenzied fit,
A soul entombed
By its own falsified concepts.
Seeks fervently
For Heaven's room,
To free itself from its own gloom.

Itself to blame,
It bows in shame
Knowing not where to hide this flame.
'Til in mire it sinks,
Darkening 'til
Even from Divine light it shrinks.

But rhapsody's
Melodious tune,
To Heaven's rapture daily plays.
To capture;
As the fisher's net,
Earth souls that too long have been lost.

And to those who pray
Know Heaven's way
Shall bless you with a finer day.
Aye, brighter mists,
Much finer trysts,
Where self-knowing souls shall dwell in peace.

ARENA TERRA

I see men.
I see men nearer to gods.
I see men nearer to gods than apes to us.

I see gods.
I see god-men from afar.
I see god-men tread the Earth with feathered
touch.

And though in wishful
Dreams am swept.
A wistful feather that has long wept -
I see god-men
Prancing thither
In delight.

Still I ponder what the
Limits be
Of this long drawn out confusing
Scene
A jovial, sometimes tragic view;
Evolution's screen.

And heaven at times drops its hints
In men that we call 'genius';
And the sages that have graced us -

Ah I see.

I see gods.
I see god-men from afar.
At evolution's limitless horizons, peer I -
And see gods.

MY QUEEN

'Tis Philosophers' Milk that did interrupt
My life
In manner so abrupt.
My mind it did seem to corrupt,
All plans for peace did swift disrupt.

And though this creative life's gentle bloom
Was attended daily, by incessant gloom,
Still - the words that from my soul did flow,
Left its basal tones
With a matchless glow.

And by my arcane alchemy,
(That secret of poets of Ancient clime)
I supped lavishly from a chalice hid
'Til, on insanity's cusp -
I was near-mad rent!

Yet Nature gentle,
Oh that sweet
And kind
Eternal mother dear,
Did uplift me to'ards Her light serene.
To bless me with this writ: my Queen.

PHOENIX RISING

Into the furnace, head-first I went,
Where even demons fear to tread.
Into the furnace, I was swift-sent
To bathe in terrors that I did dread.

And abysmal horrors did befall
My shrieking soul 'til it near fell.
Into the furnace, I did so fall
Into a dark eternal well.

But secret fire's sacred quest
Lies in that it is Mankind's final test.
Dive into the furnace - make this your conquest!
And as a twice-born phoenix, sup eternal rest.

4TH NIGHT

Verily - 'tis compassions' Rose
That aids me in my prose.
On this arduous Physician night-shift
That fails to budge 'ere swift.

Yet soft-buttered hearts,
Still leave fluttered arts
That half- sleep somehow divined.
Poesic brains
E'en when by lack of sleep strain'd,
In truth - shall never be slain.

FOLLOW NATURE

"Follow nature, follow nature", the alchemist inscribes.
"Follow nature, follow nature", the alchemist prescribes.
"Follow nature, follow nature", I repeat as a scribe -
"Follow nature, follow nature", must I offer thee a bribe?

EPIPHANY

Struggles that do strike us deep
And reveal that we are so very meek,
Do in unwary moments seep
Into our fragile hearts until we seek
Solace, comfort, peace and joy -
Calm repose, and tender rest
Where none can our fragile soul destroy
Or our strange emotional ways test.
This young poet does sit oft confused
That in false-wisdom and high conceit,
Thought he knew it all when he fast mused,
And must now take to Nature's humble seat
And know there is much more to learn
And far much more to understand;
'Tis wisdom for long, that I did yearn
And now, with love alone, at peace I stand.
Where tender angels shall forever dwell
And my healing wounds, sweet-softly kiss.
When in tears, tell me all shall be well,
"John, fight on and you'll win your eternal bliss".

FORTITUDAS

Whene'er so gravely tired thou be,
And through weary eyes can you naught see.
When life does strike you a severest blow,
And leaves you feeling sombre and low.

Know friend, that this Heaven-sent test
Is designed to spur you towards your best
And through my own trials, I can attest,
You are permitted ocassional rest.

But not so much you over lay
So the Devil may with your idle fingers play.
Life's challenges are the earth-scholar's lamp
To lead him higher up evolution's ramp.

Yet this does not all mean you will not still cry,
Nor that life will you less arduously try.
But know my good friend, that at any rate
With fortitudas, you will (I promise) make it
through Heaven's gate.

NEW AGE

The real world
Presented too painful a spectre
So the young boy -
John -
Lost himself in Poesy.
Frolicking in inner-fields of pure delight
Where nought could in his tender Soul arouse
fright.
And as he does slowly come of age,
Gazing at the Solar-Orbit's
New page,
He stumbles -
Tentative -
Before Life's stage
Calling forth a bright New-Age!

I REMEMBER

I remember how I did feel,
When to life's trials I was forced to kneel.
How I daily sat and wondered how
To wipe the sweat, from my tired brow.

I remember when harsh blows did strike
To my surprise, such endless strife!
Leaving me, but with disdain and dislike
Of this spectacle humankind calls 'life'.

I remember, in the midst of it all
It felt it would not cease, 'til I did fall.
What wretched curse had on my head befall'n
And who had I mistakenly scorned?

I remember, as if they yesterday were,
Those trials that did my emotions blur.
But though still worn, I now understand
'Twas all a part of evolution's plan.

PERSEVERANTIA

You'll face hours of melancholy,
When for days you shall so despondent be;
Trying moments when you will not even believe
There exists any valid reason to live.

Dreadful times when even the ones you love,
You'll push way with the severest shove.
Harsh actions that will confuse you so
Sinking you, to an even deeper low.

In these trials, please my friend, do not fear:
Know very well, that the Lord still flows truly near.
Persevere my friend, swim strong I pray,
For beyond every dark night, lies a new-spring day.

HE VISIONS THIS

He holds a steely gaze,
Unphased,
By the tests that before his mind's eye do rise.
A scholar
Hard-buffeted by life's trials,
Now older, far more ripened and wise.
And holds his mind aloft on high
Breathes deep, a heavy-mellow sigh.
Gazes onwards to the horizons
Crisp.
And his vision softly declares.

PEG-LEG

'Tis this once meningitis afflicted brain
The Lord planned to entrain.
To settle the score of microbial lore,
With empyrean verses galore.

And even though now partial deaf
Music, my soul doth still enchant.
Sweet harmonies, this poet sups
To rival those school-day chants.

And though I still limp,
'Cripple' once named
This lion, they could not tame.
Nor maim
Nor strain
With their fickle aim.
Aye
Seems, 'Peg-leg' - he won the day.

THE DUEL

In vain, e'en my own compatriots,
Do swift get tired of me.
When my fallen mind can't connect the dots
With a bleeding heart that fails to proper see
That though donned in Venusian attire,
Sweet maidens who graced with lotus smell,
Shall not, it seems, ever tire
From leading young poets' hearts astray.

And dreams, that were my cherished wish,
In bosom tucked away.
I dismally, watch as fate does dish
Its fiery torrential foray.
And down there casts, the sandy castles
That did my blooming mind paint
And with reality's painful touch,
The bubble burst and taints -

My naive view of this here life
Its every second, a sweltered knife.
But ever, I keep on
In manly stride
And do keep up my pride.

Yet knowing that deeper there does rest
A poet that life does test,
Witnessed anguish, 'til e'en death I fear not;
Come now life - do your best.

SENSEI'S LESSON

The only way to o'ercome a maiden's 'feeble plays'
Is with utmost utmost patience,
And highly skilful ways.

RECESS À-LA GINSBERG

Where I went to school.
Getting addicted to cigarettes at 14;
Was cool.

My brother.
He tells me that where he went to school.
Such people were thought tools;
Yes.
Fools.

Among these curious youth;
Who makes these rules?
And what are they
As grown-ups?
Cool.
Fools.
Or tools.

And what then,
My dear friend
Are you?

LOTHARIO

While in his bed he soundly slept
She - in hers - lay coiled, and wept.
Little did he know how much she still pined
For those days she's upon his chest reclined.

Around him her discomfort she'd hid
Trembling, she lovingly would gaze
Into his eyes, seeking to his concealed soul pierce
'Til love's fumes would cause hers to glaze.

But melancholy does Fortune's fate spoil
Despite meek lovers' arduous toil,
And the artists' moods, bipolar they -
Frighten lovers away.

But adamant,
She did him pursue
Her own values betrayed.
And all that in her heart she felt true
She readily from them strayed.

Knowing not that
Nature long ago decreed
That if we would experience true Joy's dew,
We must seek integrity in every deed.
And above all,
To ourselves be true.

That no man, woman, child nor friend
Must us from our path deter;
And the highest, truest
Most beauteous love,
Shall never with our pre-ordained Quest interfere.

And the true love we so ardent seek,
It must be found within.
And when for it, in the heart of others we peek,
Our own is rendered weak.

Her pillow drenched,
Mid-slumber she
Did from her pillow rise.
Swore never to so reckless be,
Faced Heavenward,
And vowed to be more wise.

INNER PAIN

Inner pain is a lesson veiled
And what it does contain,
Is the gift of wisdom,
To your soul unstain -
And true happiness unveil.

DREAMS

The dreams that once did make me reel
No longer seem so real.
Those days of youthful ecstasy;
Naive serenity.

Those visions that a joyous youth do make
Life did swift from me take;
Where are the joys of former days?
Stolen by Life's harsh ways.

Yet when in this sadness I do dwell,
A soft voice to my soul doth sing
And choir bells through my being do ring,
"All friend, shall soon be well".

THINK ON THESE THINGS

The so called 'verity' men take as facts
To keep their worlds intact.
Are dubious notions carefully wrought,
So none shall mutiny concoct.
Think not that these are here to your life serve
Remember; nothing do you innately deserve.
Beware of articles that
Inform the growth of the blossoming mind,
And then that self-same psyche by its own tenets
bind.

You speak of freedom;
How-so, my friend,
When you were in chains, born?
Yet for a lifetime
Many o'er sup fine wine
Then on their deathbed, the whole world scorn.

When all the while
True-freedom's key
Did in their own hand sit.
Is it too hard
A mental exercise
My friend,
To the wheat
From the chaff sift?

NEITHER BLACK NOR WHITE

Life it is a series of greys,
And therefore know that come what may.
At every corner that we turn,
There is still much more to learn.

FREEDOM WON

We immerse ourselves in outer play,
For fearing the journey within.
'Til rigor-mortis leaves us hard as clay
And wondering
'What could have been?'
Lives too oft lived on others terms,
Yet when we are infirm,
Those 'others' are nowhere to be found
But by their chains, still, are we bound.
Thus:
I seek a freedom higher than has been by my
schools decreed,
One higher, even, than the cherished seed
That was by my well-meaning parents instilled.
And on the day this freedom - long-sought -
Has verily been won,
I'll meticulously place those Hermian sandals
On,
Then
To the Heavens turn.
Glance back at my former estate
And vow
Never to return

THAT LION-FORCE

Those unruly thoughts
Which he'd long fought
To - in his mind
Contain.
Did torture him
'Til it did on on him dawn
They could never him, nor others
Maim.
But instead when grasped
They would him swiftly
To higher mental regions lead.
And as a hero new-born
He'd to Olympus proudly rise
With Pegasus, as his steed.

AN ODE TO MASLOW

Man has long questioned what
The Peak-Experience be.
Those transient states of fleeting joy
When his own Self he does see.
Can any one so profoundly touched
(By Heaven's fine-stroke brushed)
Ever doubt that beyond our senses be
Regions ever-more free.

Maslow he spake
Of that Empyrean lake
That he too, once did glimpse.
The pleasures of another world,
That in reality, are Within.
And William James' intellect,
This topic, its interest piqued
And a fine tome
Sprung from his cranial dome;
On 'The Varieties' of mystics' dreams.

It seems when each of us are fed,
And nursed; have rested well,
Nature compels us all the more
To find that Inner Shore.
Where gifts resplendent are to be found
Where True-Light in abundance lives.
To grace us with a wisdom deep-felt;
The rare Knowledge of one's true 'Self'.

TAT TVAM ASI

And with this Realization:
That 'I Am'
A Drop of Consciousness,
A Unit Resplendent,
A Being Infinite;
I can now
Finally
At long last
In Peace,
Rest.

'Tis not the morrow that shall save me.
Nor do I await the future to grace me.
My Heaven is here;
Paradise is now..
Matter 'tis but a
Reflection
Of the Spirit's Will.
Volition, the master of position
And conditions.
Circumstance is not an adversary
But a friend -
If I know how
To mould it.
An ally
That intends to show
Me through:
Pain (of my own doing).
Adversity (borne of my ignorance)
Suffering - or 'training'.
Whatever you wish to call it.
However you see fit.

Intends to show me
That Perennial
Strait gate
Which
Shall forever stay.

And thus,
The Great Work must never cease.
E'en in the throng
Of what is 'ere revealed;
Immortals' Play.

Ah yes - Know Thyself.

'Tis far easier said.
Than done

BESEECHED

What misery
Must meet a man,
Before he 'ttempts to reach,
To'ards the Heavens - be beseeched
To, his own Maker seek.
Must Death who does wait at Her door
Be our eternal envoy?
Must She fore'er be the unruly bait
That startles us awake?

DICHOTOMY

Though it at times can be a drain -
Love dictates the poet's brain.
And copious verses thence do flow
And raise his spirit afloat.

But modern life this passion tests
'Til left with meagre rest,
Pragmatic ways do then compete
Claiming to make life more complete.

But e'en the wealthy can attest
That any spirit left
Without a true-passion to pursue,
A life joyless will ensue.

So on the cusp of them I live;
My ideals - and believe,
That twists of fate ultimately do conspire
To quell the poet's restless fire.

THE DAY HEAVEN SPOKE

My son:
When you did in anguish lay
And towards me turned, so you could pray.
I never did you ever forsake
Or my treasures, from you then take.

My son:
When life's torrents, slings and bows.
Did into your life bring deep sorrow,
Your occasional respite was my sweet touch
At least now, you should know this much.

And my son:
Where'er you now do go,
My voice into thine eye shall flow.
My son, please know that come what may,
Your Cosmic Father shall with you, forever stay.

AN ODE TO THE MASTER ALCHEMIST

Messages descended from the supermind
Do bring fine sight, to humans blind.
And so with fine words did the Master heal
When his inspired mind did those aching hearts
feel.
But you see - 'twas never for men to before him
kneel
But to apply his wisdom, and reach the Real.

THAT GIRL

Why did this that girl I so beauteous found,
Did my naive heart - then – rend.
What scheming plot did cross her mind
What did she, friend, intend?
And though twas verse as sweet as this,
And times even more, I lent.
Was it destined still,
Or Heaven's will
That she should poniards
In return send?

'Tis such immoral acts,
That tend t'wards pacts
To never another maiden trust.
Though wisdom's song
Does whisper 'ere,
That for my own sake,
I must.

I must
Be led by finer the find
That does me to God bind.
I must not distrustful be
But beauty in all men see.
And though some may for
Me ill wish
I must love, but know when to guard.
Not seal,
But watch.
Not imprison,
But guard.
'Tis what wisdom does sing to me.

BUT A DREAM

I doubt many do understand
Where before I once did stand.
Life's turmoils did over-stretch my brain -
And it crumbled under the strain.

And faculties I once thought were mine,
I could no longer find.
And nightly would in wailful sob weep,
As tears would from my wounds seep.

Oh! the fine joy that does grace
One, on seeing a long-known friend's face,
This was a treasure I no longer knew
For my mind it no longer drew:

No longer drew the brighter days -
Those times of fairer climes.
No longer let me contemplate
The highs of finer times.
No longer
Did it draw plans for my fate,
Through which my ambition grew;
Those hours when life trials would not decrease,
Yet, my defiant will, still would increase.
Aye -
It no longer even dwelt on those mighty hopes
Of meeting that kindred soul;
This brain now charred,
My one true friend
Did me from life-sweet debar.

But:

Now- here, as that sweet-madness fades,
The past seems but a haze.
And my friend, Brain
Sings at a higher pitch
And with wisdom
Does me train.

And then those borrowed moments of Pure
Ecstasy
(A realm in which I oft dwell)
Make that horror past, now so trifle seem;
As if it all were,
But a dream.

SEA OF DIAMONDS

I saw a man in poverty
And scolded him severely.
Deep-bruised, he bared his soul to me,
And his inner diamonds, I did see.
I wondered the day aimlessly
Pond'ring on this and how,
The man I thought a beggar
Rightly, now seemed a King to me

THAT SECRET STRENGTH

Those of our age
Must rewrite the script,
We do paint of old-age.
In seeming frailty, glimpse that secret strength,
That verily marks the sage.

The 'elderly' we have named them,
But bygone eras did far more see.
Did not the wisdom of these wise elders,
Light all our wilderness
With rare tenderness.

The sun it sets in the evening whence
It does upon its earlier moments reflect.
To arise on another day,
And grander worlds erect.
We are that early morning sun,
The boisterous fiery son.
But they - the serene one of dusk,
Whose true life has only just begun.

PART IV

LIGHT

The rays of divine light upon our lips, we are energised once more by this natural sustenance. Our mind, body, heart and soul are filled with an indescribable joy welling from within. We are humbled to the ground by the witnessed glory. The apprehension of the light occurs sporadically but each new experience of it is stronger and of a longer duration. Insights descend. Clarity dawns. We slowly begin to understand our place and part in the cosmic scheme. We are gradually stripped of conditioned desires until only one ambition remains: to become a more fitting instrument for the expression of the Limitless 'Splendour Within'. And one goal: to actively love, and then love even greater still. In peace at long last from the existential agony, a new apprentice stands upright and marches on...

IMMORTAL DEEDS

Immortal deeds are never done
Where calmness alone does resound.
Where minds cannot e'en themselves stretch
And in the Heavens etch.

Immortal words are never writ
By the souls of the o'er meek;
Would Achilles' name modern ears meet
If he had been in spirit weak?

Immortal deeds, friends
Are the marks
Of waking eternal sparks -
Who've wrestled life's torrential seas
To summon eternities - for posterity
And thee.

LESSONS OF HADES

I bear the wounds inflicted by an unhinged Mind
That anger did firmly bind;
Psychological machinations towards me wrought,
Against which I fervently fought.

With frenzied Will
I grasped until
My Spirit did sorely pain.
Respite at last found -
Or so I thought -
'Til fiercely, it advanced again.

When in spirit rendered weak,
The human psyche
Does power through brute-force seek.
Restless constructs despairing
For loss of love,
Temporal replenishment hastily drink.

But inner peace,
That edifice -
Even in times of the most arduous strain -
With the steady guide that is our Inward Voice,
Marks Love true as our most noble choice.

TOMORROW'S MAN

A man must be able to spar
And compute distance of far-away star.
Yield when he will, a writer's pen
Yet with bare hands, ward off beasts in lion's den.

Sew threaded gold 'pon linen silk,
Sweet song for his fair girl compose.
Hard work, nay, must he never shirk
But crown it with Adonisian pose.

Carve beauties from raw chiselled stone,
That'll grace the streets, as in long gone Rome.
And as in Grecian senate, rivals oppose,
Then dance with numerals in his sweet night
repose.

A man should be this and so much more,
Yet not be tempted when summoned, 'encore'.
Seek solace in serenity,
And sweet rest in his own company.

With Athenian mind must he be bless'd,
And Spartan sculpt sublimely dressed;
Who'll submit not, e'en to his own selfish whim
Show me tomorrow's man - that'll be him!

KNOW THIS

Know that man is destined to rise
Beyond intellect, and to be more wise.
Know that it was long ago decreed
That he shall be, from mortal fetters freed.

Know his evolutionary sojourn is planned
Please take your time, to this understand;
The Great Architect a high-genius be
And works in ways we cannot even see.

Know this and please know even more
That you are loved - of this please be sure.
The future's forecast, 'tis not full of gloom
And this Earth-orchard shall one day, with high-
Sages bloom.

HYPERSPACE; OR, THE MUSIC OF THE SPHERES

Where would I be without the Super(conscious)
mind
From whence all true arts are found.
I shudder to think of the arduous grind
To which my writ would be daily bound.

It seems expressive arts
Are but the minute parts
Of a Grand-Mind in Sweet Rhapsody.
Electric whorls,
The fecund of magnetic worlds -
Aye; 'tis Pythagoras' audible-physics symphony!

AMBROSIA

My Life be like the spider's web
Entwined in rhapsody.
Soaked in Heaven's sweet liquor
That upon it glides, and makes it gleam.

APPRENTICED TO THEE

Though the poetic form be an art that all can see,
Far more for than a pastime it be.
Did Creation spring from One who had
Exhausted all to do but 'be'?
Did Shakespeare's pen, that once sonnets sang,
Do so when by solitude harangued;
What stroke of Fate must meet the man
Who in boredom does with high-genius write?
And Keats, that noble Prince of us all,
Who posthumously, still has the world enthralled -
Did he Sirs, abandon the healing arts
To adopt as a mere hobby, this Noble craft?
I write as one who apprenticed is
To Nature, and all her beauties sweet.
In honour of my vocation do I pen this note:
Loyal to Poesy, now and forever more.

SACRED DUTY

The task of the Poet
Is to convey
In one verse
What would require many books to say.

When dashed upon Life's harsh precipice
He strives on to'ards True Love's peace.

The Poet - as the martyr -
He does not feign,
His works thus, are never written in vain.

And when he does to the Infinite leap,
Upon the mortal page,
He infuses his Spirit to load and bless
Yet another Age.

THE POET'S CLOVER

Who hath tasteth that Freedom sweet,
Enchanted regions of unbounded inner-space?
Beckoned sweet hymns plucked from starry planes,
And watched as Heaven settled at thy very feet.

One enchanting petal present to thine Queen;
'Til all the faeries of Earth thrill to her name.
The second a token to thine Creator whom,
To poets in their inner travels speaks.

The third to thine sweet mother kind
Oh – how rare, gems as her are to find.
The fourth, to thine brothers and Father both;
Veritable Princes of Honour sublime!

SMALL 'p' pHILOSOPHY

Small 'p' philosophy is a callous phantasy,
That makes for naught, but for supper pleasantry.
Writ by those who wise airs pretend,
When to crush hearts, is what they intend.
My friend, if it is wisdom you seek,
Test a poet's pen; it is ever so meek.
And it does towards sweet love incline
So that yours and your lover's hearts shall like ivy
entwine.

J'ESPÈRE

When I am old, and of poetic verses spent,
Grey haired, frail-skinned and nearing death.
When all has flowed that God intends to send
On this poetic youth's love-bitten bed.
I pray these words shall by then have reached
The future youth, and the truth leaked
That God in in their very own souls be.

UNROOTED

The winds of life upturn many trees
With a gust that only those with the deepest roots
can withstand.
They do for this reason beyond mortal gaze lie:
Even all of Solomon's wealth could not this
immortal treasure buy.

AN EPIPHANY

The Lord would never tell thee
Where he has your soulmate hid,
Even if you did with him
Bid.
What suffering does mortal man
Hap'ly endure
To 'precious' clod secure.

Yet in the realm of Spirit these
Mighty efforts
Do absurdly cease.
He forgets that
Such a high-prize does not exist,
To indolent man, mere appease.

Oh - He does amuse
For he reckons that
Pure love, can be found with ease.
Aye:
The earth is not an arena where
He can - without a price - receive as it does him
please.

SWEET FREEDOM, RING!

Let Freedom - that sweet star ablaze -
Kiss our foreheads when Heavenward we gaze.
Let it be the balm that tenderly
Caresses us, when we do our loved ones miss.

Freedom that martyrs from rooftops did chant.
Naught else they did but this nectar want.
Let it form the mould of our cherished dreams,
Upon which palaces we shall build.

Let freedom that did wipe my tears
When I laid, overcome by my fears.
Let that sweet nurse whisper into thine ear,
"My child, keep hope, thine light be near".

Let her - in your moments of doubt -
Slip truth into thine inner mind.
Let it teach you how to be kind,
For Freedom teaches compassion rare to find.

Let Freedom that for so long man has sought.
That e'en with diamonds can ne'er be bought.
Let Liberation ring and herenow declare
'His' children's handiwork below the firmament.

SELF-COMPASSION

What misty thoughts do haunt the minds of life-
carers on their shifts.
To what lonely regions of the human psyche do
physicians daily drift.
To tenderly, provide affection to those in whom life
ails,
It be our mission and our noble task,
But we must not our own selves fail.

MY NIRVANAS

Mortal men are rarely free
I hope this, you do friend see.
Oft defeated minds that have long festered lain,
'Til their weakness is to all made plain.
Yet how do I now reconcile
This -
With the darkness that seems to fill our globe -
And keep high-hopes as my seed.

It is because when life's trials were sent
It was to Hell I went.
Awoke to find that all was lost,
Things I then deemed to be of great cost.
But then remembered the Immortal Bliss
That one day
Into my mind
Did shine; a Light that had set me free.
And I lie not -
My soul sang high-songs even in the midst of
gloom,
To once more, sup serenity's bloom.

SUBTERFUGE

How modern scientific subterfuge
Does religious doctrines judge,
Is conceit that does my brain astound
With its hypocritical-filled jargon abound.
What ill caprice can render Karmic-Justice
To be ever less,
That Heaven's bountiful tenderness
That does us mere mortal men bless.

No mere human flight,
Can overstep
And reach that ingenious might.
Whose sights
Can reach beyond clear skies,
To sup intuitive delights.
Reserved it seems but to the few
Yet - all men are in time, destined to view
Horizons that escape modern's man gaze;
And yet, e'en the immortals daze.

And with this pen
I dare
Declare
That those two 'foes' shall on a future day be one
To Religion-science, Nature doth intend,
To one day nuptial gifts send.

AN ODE TO NATURE

Feed me my friend
And be my breath
Unto, my very death.
Feed me with fine poetic writ
When I do, in anguish sit.
Feed me, dear friend
When my soul doth ache,
When I feel the need to brake -
Those times when I have thought over-long,
And fail to hear Life's song.
Feed those wounds, and pass as gold
Through my veins
When'er I do live in vain.
Friend, Mammon with you, I know competes -
But e'en then, do me with wisdom, feed.
Feed me even if you must into me drill
Knowledge, so I may be still.
Lend me thine, Art
Oh, dearest friend -
And never from me depart.

POETS ARISE!

They thought I'd cower sheepishly
When they called us Poets
Weak.
So I did heavier dumbbells seek
'Til a sculptured physique they did see.
Poets - for their glory -friends,
Have waited far too long.
And now the Heavens beckon us
To proudly sing our song!

SUN-TUITION

A poet did Love contemplate
As the day lingered late,
The enigma of all Ages
That has a thousand miles of pages
Filled.

And as he watched that golden orb fall,
It did upon him dawn:
Love, it is man's very essence
And its expression life's purpose be

ON TRUE MARRIAGE

Why implore them,
"To love and to cherish
'Til death doth do us part".
When e'en Death has never severed
The most true of lovers' hearts.

A PRAYER

Father:
Give me strength,
That I may serve
And never be unnerved.
Give your child an unwavering Faith
So That He may do your will.
Give me a heart that can stay still,
And so unruffled, other men Heal.
Give me that imperturbable Inner Peace
That not even earthly gold can match.
Give me Compassion - Oh my Lord -
Let light from my being stream.
Give me forgiveness
So I humbly can,
Make my neighbours' burdens less.
Vest me with Truth
Immutable,
Let my actions be the proof,
That a Higher Being, verily lives
And readily forgives.
My actions and tongue Lord - saturate both -
With Honey from above,
May what I say
And what I do
Today, my Lord
Reflect Your Light, in me.

OUR HARVEST,

Or; Lyrics for Wondrous Times

From inner effort
Doth spring inner joy,
The fruits of moments wisely spent.
When Heaven did Cupid beckon
A young Poet did all his forces summon
And was swift -
With Sophia -
To Paradise sent!

THE ALCHEMIST; OR,
AUTOBIOGRAPHY OF A POET

I did long seek that 'peace profound'
Wondering where it should be found.
Sought for it in my travels far
In sandcastles built afar.
Searched humankind's vast libraries;
Through numerous tomes I pored -
'Til racked, my brain, did overstretch,
And life - swift - was shipwrecked.
Defiant, I looked further still,
"It lies in solving Mankind's ills".
But elusive sweet serenity
Did never visit me.
I loved
And prayed that love's return,
Would quench my agony.
In sweet embrace, did seek peace of mind,
But instead, lost my mind!
Exhausted, I summoned posthumous rest;
My true and honest friend.
In self-pity, I peered within
And lo! There, found my gold.

ABOUT THE AUTHOR

John FW Ndikum is a medical doctor who composed his first published poem at the age of thirteen. He went on to win the Bedfordshire section of the Future Writers (Remus House) poetry competition at the age of seventeen, securing £2,000 for his sixth form in the process.

An intense period of introspection in his early twenties plunged him into the depths of his psychological world, resulting in an unexpected phase of prolific creative output.

He emerged from this inner journey with numerous poems as his prize and a greater clarity about his place and purpose in the world. It is his hope that those who shall find themselves in a similar position, may find peace, comfort and inspiration in his words.

John's continued dedication to improving the health of populations has led him to Yale School of Public Health, where he will commence his studies in July 2017. In the Spring of the same year, he will be getting married to his fiancée and love of his life, Sophie Wickham.

He currently lives in Hertfordshire, England, where he continues his vocational work as a junior physician in Internal Medicine.

Lightning Source UK Ltd.
Milton Keynes UK
UKOW01n1432250916

283767UK00001BA/4/P